Skelfie and the Spookeville Circus

By
Lilli Adams

Skelfie and the Spookeville Circus

© Copyright 2025 - All rights reserved.

The content contained within this book may not be reproduced, duplicated or transmitted without direct written permission from the author or the publisher.

Under no circumstances will any blame or legal responsibility be held against the publisher, or author, for any damages, reparation, or monetary loss due to the information contained within this book, either directly or indirectly.

Legal Notice:

This book is copyright protected. It is only for personal use. You cannot amend, distribute, sell, use, quote or paraphrase any part, or the content within this book, without the consent of the author or publisher.

Disclaimer Notice:

Please note the information contained within this document is for educational and entertainment purposes only. All effort has been executed to present accurate, up to date, reliable, complete information. No warranties of any kind are declared or implied. Readers acknowledge that the author is not engaged in the rendering of legal, financial, medical or professional advice. The content within this book has been derived from various sources. Please consult a licensed professional before attempting any techniques outlined in this book.

By reading this document, the reader agrees that under no circumstances is the author responsible for any losses, direct or indirect, that are incurred as a result of the use of the information contained within this document, including, but not limited to, errors, omissions, or inaccuracies.

Lilli Adams

Dedication

This book is dedicated to intergenerational relationships and to one very special and much-loved Poppy who laughed out loud at his own jokes.

Acknowledgment

This book acknowledges children's rights to be playful, creative and to have fun. We acknowledge diverse cultural practices and hope that sharing in each other's traditions and customs brings joy.

Table of Contents

Dedication	iii
Acknowledgment	iv
Prologue: Visiting My Grandparents	6
Day 1: October 18th	10
Day 2: October 19th	13
Day 3: October 20th	16
Day 4: October 21st	18
Day 5: October 22nd	21
Day 6: October 23rd	24
Day 7: October 24th	27
Day 8: October 25th	30
Day 9: October 26th	33
Day 10: October 27th	35
Day 11: October 28th	38
Day 12: October 29th	40
Day 13: October 30th	43
Day 14: October 31st - Halloween	46
Epilogue: November 1st - All Saints' Day	51

Prologue:
Visiting My Grandparents

Ella and I sat in the back seat of Dad's car, watching the city melt into long stretches of trees and rolling hills. The air outside felt lighter here, brighter somehow, and even though we had hours to go, I didn't mind. This trip was going to be different—a break from everything I knew about school, routines, and homework.

Ella had a book balanced on her knees, of course. She was already lost in it and didn't even look up when Dad tried one of his jokes—something about skeletons and "nobody" caring.

Grandpa would've laughed. Grandpa laughed at everyone's bad jokes.

I had a book on my lap too, but I wasn't studying. Before we left, Mum had handed me something—a small notebook with a soft, black cover.

"This is for you," she said, placing it in my hands.

"What for?" I flipped through the blank pages.

"For writing down everything that happens during the trip," she explained. "This is a special time with Grandma and Grandpa, and I don't want you to forget a single moment. Write about the fun stuff, the weird stuff, even the boring stuff. You can share it with me when we get back."

"You want me to write every day?" I groaned.

"Just a little," she said with a smile. "Think of it like your own storybook. You'll be glad you did when it's over."

I looked at the notebook again. It did feel kind of cool, like it was waiting for something amazing to be written inside.

"Fine," I said, tucking it into my backpack so I wouldn't forget to pack it later.

And just like that, I had my first homework assignment for the trip. But maybe it wouldn't feel like homework at all.

"Are you two excited to see Grandma and Grandpa?" Mum asked now from the front seat, twisting to look at us. She looked tired but happy, her work bag wedged between her feet like it was too full to zip.

"Yeah," I said, leaning my forehead against the cool window. "Grandma's going to bake biscuits, right?"

"I'm sure she's planning to spoil you," Mum said.

Skelfie and the Spookeville Circus

I couldn't wait! Plus, it was October, and my grandparents went all out for Halloween. Ella and I had never seen their decorations in person, only in the faded photos Mum kept in an album.

I really wanted to see the infamous "Skelfie" from the old Halloween photos of Uncle Ben. In one picture, he was holding the little skeleton toy, grinning like he'd just pulled off a prank. Apparently, Grandma had made Skelfie one Halloween, stitching him together from leftover fabric after making Uncle Ben's ringmaster costume. But the best part was the stories. According to Mum, Skelfie used to get up to all kinds of mischief in the days leading up to Halloween—moving around the house, hiding lollies, and playing little pranks.

"Of course," Mum would say, rolling her eyes, "it wasn't really Skelfie. It was just Ben being his usual annoying little brother self."

But looking at the faded photos, I wasn't so sure. Skelfie had this cheeky grin stitched on his face, like he really could be planning something. And now, staying in Uncle Ben's old room, I couldn't help but wonder: would Skelfie still be up to his old tricks?

"Are you nervous about staying for two weeks?" Dad asked, pulling into a servo to fill up.

"Nope," I said quickly.

"Maybe a little," Ella said, snapping her book shut. "I just hope the Wi-Fi works. I've got a research paper due."

Of course, my sister would be worried about school. She was in high school and very serious about getting into a good uni. I was in primary school and hated thinking about the years of school stretching out before me. I knew I'd have to do remote learning while I was with my grandparents, but I was trying to view the whole thing as a holiday from my usual life.

Dad chuckled. "They ran speed tests on their internet and trust me, you're in good hands. Your grandparents have been looking forward to this for weeks."

When we finally pulled into their driveway, Grandpa was already there, waving from the verandah. Lola, their little dachshund, yapped and spun in circles at his feet like she couldn't decide which of us to greet first.

"Well, look who it is!" Grandpa called. His voice was as warm as his hugs, and when he scooped me up, I could feel the scratch of his jumper against my cheek. "You're just in time. We've got big plans for Halloween this year."

"Big plans?" Ella asked, raising an eyebrow.

Grandpa winked. "You'll see."

It was going to be an October to remember.

Skelfie and the Spookeville Circus

Day 1: October 18th

This morning, I woke up to the smell of pancakes and the sound of Grandpa humming off-key in the kitchen. Breakfast was great—Grandma made pancakes shaped like ghosts and bats, and I ate three of them before Grandpa had even finished his first one.

After brekkie, I headed to my room to get dressed. Grandma had laid out my clothes on the dresser the night before, just like she said she would. It felt nice having someone else think about what I was going to wear for once. I decided to wear my favourite socks—the ones with the racing cars zooming across the ankles. They were right on top of the pile last night.

But when I reached for them, they were gone.

I froze, staring at the empty spot on the dresser where my socks should've been. The rest of my clothes were still there, folded neatly, but the socks had vanished.

"Grandma?" I called out, running to the kitchen. "Did you move my socks?"

Grandma looked up from the sink where she was rinsing dishes. "Your socks? No, sweetheart, I haven't touched them. Are you sure they're not in your room?"

"I just checked!" I said. "They were on the dresser, but now they're gone."

Grandma wiped her hands on a tea towel and smiled. "Let's go have a look, shall we?"

We searched my room from top to bottom. Grandma checked under the bed while I rummaged through the drawers, even though I knew I hadn't put them there. I checked my suitcase and then double-checked, just in case the socks had magically reappeared. No luck.

"They couldn't have just disappeared," Grandma said, frowning. "Let's try the lounge room."

We looked everywhere—under the couch cushions, behind the curtains, even inside the pantry, just in case I'd absentmindedly carried them there. Nothing.

That's when Grandma had an idea. "Let's check Lola's kennel," she said.

"Why would my socks be in there?" I asked, following her to the corner of the kitchen where Lola's little bed was tucked under the counter.

"Lola's been known to take things," Grandma said, crouching down. "She's a sneaky little thing when she wants to be."

Sure enough, there they were—my racing car socks, crumpled in a ball right in the middle of Lola's bed.

"Lola!" I groaned, holding up the socks. "Why would you take these?"

Lola sat on the floor nearby, looking up at me with her big brown eyes. She tilted her head to one side, wagged her tail, and gave the smallest bark.

"She's cheeky, that one," Grandma said with a laugh, scratching Lola behind the ears.

"But how?" I said, staring at the socks. "She's so short she can't even get on the couch. How did she get them off the dresser?"

Lola gave me a sideways glance, like she knew something I didn't.

"I don't know," Grandma said, taking the socks from me and inspecting them. "Maybe they fell off, and she grabbed them."

"But they didn't fall," I insisted. "I remember putting them on top of the pile. There's no way she could've reached."

Grandma shrugged, smiling. "Well, it's a mystery then."

I looked at Lola, who was still wagging her tail like she'd just won a prize. She caught my eye and gave me the most mischievous look I'd ever seen from a dog.

I gave her my best side-eye in return, and for a second, I thought I saw her smirk.

This wasn't over.

But I didn't have time to start a war with a dog just then. I still had to do my schoolwork, even though I didn't want to. I knew my teachers would contact my parents if I didn't, and there was no way I wanted to ruin my time at my grandparents' place.

I had to do a spelling quiz online, which was supposed to be "quick and fun," according to my teacher.

It wasn't.

I couldn't figure out how to spell *convenient* even after trying three different ways, and then the computer marked my score as *average*. Thanks a lot, computer.

While I was trying to get over my defeat, Ella came in and said she'd gotten an A on her English test. Grandma said I should "look up to my sister more," but all I wanted to do was look out the window at Grandpa and Lola digging holes in the garden. Hey, I wonder why Lola needs all those holes. What's she trying to hide? I wished my assignment could be solving that mystery.

Day 2: October 19th

Grandpa started planning *Spookeville* today. *Spookeville* is what he calls his front yard Halloween display, and he's making a wooden sign for it. Every time he says *"Spookeville,"* he uses this goofy, "spooky" voice, like a ghost with a bad cold. It's impossible not to laugh because he cracks himself up every single time.

Grandma thinks it's lame and rolls her eyes. "You're going to scare the neighbourhood kids with that voice more than your decorations!"

Skelfie and the Spookeville Circus

Grandpa just grinned and said, "Exactly!" before laughing so hard he nearly spilled his coffee. Ella and I couldn't help but giggle.

Ella helped him sketch out where all the decorations would go—tombstones in the flowerbeds, cobwebs in the bushes, and a big witch's cauldron on the porch.

Luckily, my socks didn't disappear last night. But something even weirder happened. Before I went to bed, I left my two favourite Marvel figures—Iron Man and Spider-Man—standing on my dresser. When I woke up, they were gone.

At first, I thought maybe Ella moved them as a joke, but she was too busy reading her biology book to prank me. Grandma helped me look all over the house. I checked under my bed, inside my backpack, and even in my sock drawer. Nothing.

Finally, I went downstairs to check the lounge room, and there they were. Both of them. Taped together with a strip of clear tape. And where were they? Inside Lola's kennel!

Grandma laughed when I showed her. "Oh, you must've left them outside yesterday. Lola probably thought they were her new toys," she said.

"Outside?" I frowned. "I didn't take them outside."

Grandma patted me on the shoulder and went back to folding the washing, but I stared at Lola, who was sitting by her kennel, wagging her tail like she'd just solved a mystery.

"Really, Lola?" I asked, crossing my arms. She blinked at me and tilted her head like she didn't have a clue what I was talking about.

Just like when my socks went missing, I knew there was no way Lola could've reached my dresser. Her legs are still too short and they couldn't grow tall enough and then shrink back down overnight. I couldn't help but imagine Lola wobbling around on tiny dachshund-sized stilts, her little legs moving like a wind-up toy as she reached up to snatch my Marvel figures off the dresser. The picture in my head was so ridiculous I actually started laughing out loud.

Grandpa gave me a curious look, and I waved him off, saying, "Just imagining Lola as a very ambitious thief."

Okay, I knew there was no way she'd be teetering around the house on stilts, but the picture was too funny not to smile about. Or maybe Spider-Man had helped, shooting web so she could swing from place to place until she made it to the top of the dresser and safely back down again. Silly, I know. But the fact was, somehow my Marvel figures had ended up in her kennel.

Later, Grandma said I must've forgotten where I put them. Maybe she's right. Or maybe something strange is going on in this house. I don't know. But I'm going to keep an eye on Lola.

Just in case.

Day 3: October 20th

Something strange happened again today. Grandpa had made this big, wooden *Spookeville* sign for his Halloween decorations, and he asked me to keep it safe in my room last night. "I'll finish painting it tomorrow," he said, setting it carefully on my dresser. "Just don't let it out of your sight!"

"Okay, Grandpa," I said, feeling pretty important.

But when I woke up this morning, the sign was gone.

At first, I thought maybe Grandpa had taken it with him to work on early, but when I asked him, his eyebrows shot up. "What do you mean it's gone?" he said, putting down his coffee. "That sign doesn't have legs!"

"Neither did my Marvel figures," I muttered.

"Well, actually, they do," Grandpa pointed out, and we both laughed so hard tears came to our eyes. But then we got to work.

Grandpa and I searched my room from top to bottom. Nothing. Grandpa scratched his head and said, "Well, maybe Lola borrowed it for her Halloween costume."

I laughed, but then I stopped. "Do you think it could actually be Lola?"

Grandpa shrugged. "If it is, she's a clever little thing. Let's check her favourite spots."

We looked all over the house, but we didn't see the sign anywhere.

"Grab your shoes and let's go outside. There are plenty more places to check out there."

As we stepped outside to check the yard, I suddenly remembered something about Lola. Over the past few days, I'd seen her digging a lot of holes in the garden. At first, I thought she was burying her little chew toys. And she obviously loves getting into my things. I figured she wanted some hiding spots for my socks and action figures. But what if she wasn't just hiding toys this time?

What if she was digging the holes for something else—like to help Grandpa with his *Spookeville* decorations? Maybe she had been sneaking out the sign piece by piece to set it up in her own secret way. It sounded a little crazy, but with Lola, you never really knew.

After checking the front yard, we went through the gate to check the backyard. As soon as we rounded the house, I spotted something sticking out from behind Lola's kennel.

"Grandpa!" I called.

He hurried over, and we both crouched down. There it was—the *Spookeville* sign, wedged between the back of Lola's kennel and the fence. A corner of it was chewed, and there were little paw prints smudged across the paint.

Grandpa groaned. "Lola! What have you done?"

Lola trotted up to us, wagging her tail like she was proud of herself. She barked once and then plonked down on the grass, looking completely innocent.

"I don't think she likes *Spookeville*," I said, trying not to laugh.

Grandpa sighed and picked up the sign. "Well, it's nothing a bit of paint can't fix," he said, brushing off the dirt. Then he wagged his finger at Lola. "You've got some nerve, young lady! This isn't for chewing—it's art!"

Lola barked again, like she didn't care.

We brought the sign back inside, and Grandpa started fixing it up. But now I'm starting to wonder—how is Lola getting into my room?

I think she's hiding something.

Day 4: October 21st

Something really weird happened last night. After all the work we did helping Grandpa sort through Halloween decorations—pulling out fake cobwebs, untangling lights, and dusting off his giant plastic spider—I was so tired I barely made it to bed.

I was so tired I didn't even bother taking my glass of water back to the kitchen. I just left it on my dresser next to my lamp before collapsing into bed.

This morning, when I woke up, the glass wasn't empty. It had flowers in it.

Lilli Adams

Not just any flowers either—bright orange and yellow ones. They were bunched together, sticking out of the glass like it was a vase.

At first, I thought I was still dreaming. I rubbed my eyes and stared at them for a long time. The water was still there, and I could see the ends of the stems floating just under the surface.

I ran to Ella's room and knocked on the door. "Ella! You have to see this!"

She opened the door, already holding a book in her hand like she'd been reading since dawn. "What is it now?"

"There are flowers in my water glass!"

Ella sighed and followed me back to my room. She didn't look impressed.

"See?" I said, pointing to the glass.

She stared at it for a second and then rolled her eyes. "You probably put those in there last night and forgot," she said.

"I didn't! I was too tired!"

Ella raised one eyebrow. "Are you sure? You did think you saw the moon glowing green the other night, remember?"

"That was different!" I said. "And it *was* glowing green!"

Ella shrugged. "Maybe you sleepwalked." She picked up the glass and sniffed the flowers. "They're just marigolds. Grandma probably has a hundred of these in her garden."

"Why would Grandma sneak into my room to put flowers in a glass of water?" I asked.

Skelfie and the Spookeville Circus

Ella didn't have an answer for that, so she just handed me the glass and walked out of the room, mumbling something about needing to study.

But I know I didn't put those flowers in the glass. I would have remembered doing something like that. Right?

I think something strange is going on in this house. Maybe it's Lola again. Or maybe... it's Skelfie.

To make things even stranger, I had to write a paragraph about photosynthesis for science. *Photosynthesis?* After waking up to flowers in my water glass? Tell me that's not strange!

My paragraph was supposed to explain how plants turn sunlight into energy, but honestly, I feel like plants could've kept that secret to themselves. I mean, why do I need to know about chlorophyll when all I care about is that grass is green? And solving the mystery of how Grandma's marigolds got picked and put into a water glass beside my bed.

Meanwhile, Ella was next to me with her nose buried in a biology textbook, scribbling notes like her life depended on it. Grandma walked by and said, "Look at how focused your sister is! You could take a page out of her book."

I'd rather have a nap, honestly. These missing items and mysteries are wearing me out. But if I *did* have a nap, who knows what would happen while I'm asleep!

Lilli Adams

Day 5: October 22nd

My reading assignment today was to finish a chapter of a book I don't even like and write a summary. Why does everything have to end in writing something? The book's about a boy who has to move to a new town and make new friends, but all he does is talk about how hard his life is. I wanted to tell my teacher that *my* life is hard too—because I'm stuck reading about *his* boring life while Grandpa and Lola are outside playing fetch. I bet Lola doesn't have to write summaries about boring books.

Anyway, I had the best idea ever for Halloween after I finished my classwork. Grandpa had come inside from playing with Lola in the yard. She ran to drink some water from her bowl like she'd never been so thirsty. The noise of her lapping up the water made me laugh so hard, I almost forgot about the boring assignment I had to do earlier.

Then it got even better once Grandpa and I were sitting at the kitchen table, munching on some of Grandma's choc chip biscuits (still warm from the oven). That was when it hit me—why not make this year's *Spookeville* theme a circus?

"*Spookeville Circus!*" I said, almost spraying crumbs everywhere.

Grandpa paused mid-bite, his eyebrows raising over his glasses. "Now *that*," he said, pointing his biscuit at me like it was a wand, "is a million-dollar idea."

He leaned back in his chair and called out to Grandma, who was folding towels in the laundry. "Martha, dig out those old ringmaster costumes from the attic! Looks like we've got ourselves a circus to run!"

Grandma poked her head around the corner, her hands on her hips. "You mean the ones I made for you and Ben a hundred years ago?"

"Not *that* long ago," Grandpa grumbled, but then he winked at me.

Skelfie and the Spookeville Circus

After lunch, Grandpa and I went to the garage to dig out the big box of Halloween decorations. The box was huge—almost as tall as me—and covered in cobwebs that definitely weren't fake. Grandpa said it added "authenticity" to the Halloween spirit.

Inside, we found all sorts of stuff: plastic jack-o'-lanterns, a string of ghost-shaped lights that still worked (even Grandpa looked surprised), and a rubber bat with one wing missing. And... Skelfie! Seeing him in person was so much better than hearing about his antics from Mum and Uncle Ben.

He had a stitched grin and his little ringmaster's jacket. His tiny skeleton hands were curled as if ready to hold something, and the details Grandma had sewn into his face made him look cheeky, like he was planning something mischievous. For a moment, it felt like he was looking back at me, even though I knew he was just a toy.

It was like he had a spark of magic in him, as if he was ready to come alive and join in the fun. Grandpa must've seen the way I was staring because he chuckled.

"Skelfie's got a lot of charm, hasn't he?" Grandpa said. "He's just a toy, but your Uncle Ben used to swear Skelfie had powers—like he'd sneak around at night causing trouble."

I laughed, but as I held Skelfie, I couldn't help but feel a little thrill, like anything was possible with him in my hands. After all, things had already been a bit strange during this stay... and it was just beginning.

Then Grandpa said, "Okay, let's take inventory to see what we've already got before we make a shopping list. Can't have a circus without a plan!"

We grabbed some paper and crayons and sat cross-legged on the lounge room floor. Grandpa handed me the purple crayon—he said it was "spooky" enough for a circus theme—and we started sketching out the front yard.

"We can put the big top here," I said, circling the driveway with the crayon.

Grandpa nodded. "Good. And the lolly stand can go by the front door. Maybe a ticket booth here, by the letterbox?"

"Oh! And we can use those old hula hoops in the garage for a flaming hoop jump!" I said.

Grandpa raised his eyebrows. "You planning to train Lola to jump through it?"

We both laughed, and Lola barked from her little bed in the corner, wagging her tail like she was ready to give it a go.

By the time Grandma came back downstairs with the ringmaster costumes, we had a whole plan laid out. She spread the costumes on the couch, and wow, they looked old. The jackets had faded and the gold trim was coming loose in some places, but they made me think of something I'd seen recently... Skelfie!

"Well," Grandma said, brushing dust off the sleeves, "these are going to need a lot of love before they're circus-ready."

"They'll be perfect," Grandpa said, giving her a quick kiss on the cheek. "Nothing a little magic—uh, thread and needle—can't fix."

Grandma laughed. "That's a job for tomorrow. You two clowns already have plenty to do today."

We spent the rest of the arvo going through the decorations and making lists of what we needed. Grandpa said we'd go shopping tomorrow. I can't wait to see the store—it's going to be like a treasure hunt for spooky circus stuff.

Spookeville Circus is going to be amazing.

Day 6: October 23rd

Today was the big shopping day for our *Spookeville Circus*! Grandpa said if we were going to do this, we were going to do it right, and that meant we needed supplies. First thing after brekkie (and after Lola had her morning treat—she's seriously spoiled), we loaded into Grandpa's car.

Ella sat in the back with me, her laptop open as usual, trying to finish off some assignment. I told her to take a break since this was supposed to be fun, but she just said, "Not everyone can coast through school, you know." Whatever.

Lilli Adams

Our first stop was the big craft shop. Grandpa handed me and Ella each a shopping basket and said, "Let's split up! Grab anything that screams circus—or screams in general!"

That was all I needed to hear! I raced down the aisles, picking up anything that caught my eye: spooky purple and orange fabric, glittery ribbon, and a pack of creepy fake spiders. I grabbed a clown nose for Grandpa and a big feather boa for Lola because, let's face it, she's a diva and would probably love it. Or try to eat it…

Grandpa met us by the checkout, his basket overflowing with stuff. He'd found striped paper for tickets, plastic chains for a "spooky cage," and this amazing string of lights that looked like tiny jack-o'-lanterns.

Ella added a few things too, like gold paint and some mini pumpkins. She was quieter than usual, but when I asked her about it, she said she was trying to think of how we could turn the front verandah into a big top. Honestly, sometimes I think her brain works even faster than mine, which is saying something.

Next, we went to a party supply shop. This place was awesome. They had everything from fake moustaches to skeleton hand serviettes. Grandpa picked out a giant black cauldron to use as the "popcorn stand," even though I pointed out that witches don't belong in circuses. He just winked and said, "Who's to say they don't attend once in a while?"

Finally, we hit the Halloween shop, which was my favourite stop. The entire place was decorated with animatronics that jumped and screamed, and I nearly fell over when a zombie popped out of a coffin. Ella laughed and said, "It's like you've never been in a Halloween shop before," but she jumped too when a creepy clown started laughing behind her.

I wanted to buy everything, but Grandpa said we had to stick to what we really needed. In the end, we got a fog machine, a box of glow-in-

Skelfie and the Spookeville Circus

the-dark paint, and a skeleton hand that Grandpa said could hold up the *"Welcome to Spookeville Circus"* sign.

When we got back, Grandma came out to see what we'd bought and shook her head at the pile. "You're turning this house into a funhouse," she said, but I could tell she was smiling. She took the fabric and ribbon I'd picked out, saying she'd use it to fix up the old ringmaster costumes.

The rest of the arvo was spent sorting through everything we'd bought. Grandpa and I worked on setting up the lights in the front yard, and Ella sketched out a plan for how the "big top" would look. She even figured out how to use the fog machine to make it look like there was a mysterious "beast" hiding in one of the cages.

Halloween wasn't just about lollies this year—it was about making something together. Even Ella, who usually acted like she was too cool for stuff like this, seemed to be having fun.

Now, if only Lola doesn't decide to bury the fog machine in the yard, we'll be all set.

Day 7: October 24th

This morning, Ella was at the kitchen table with her books spread out like she was preparing for a final exam. "I'll just catch up on everything today while you all go to the pumpkin patch," she announced. "It's important to stay on track."

Grandma looked up from her knitting with a raised eyebrow. "Ella, you've been studying non-stop since you got here. It's Sunday! That means it's time for a break."

Grandpa chimed in, "The pumpkin patch is a family tradition! Your Mum and Uncle Ben never missed it. You'll regret it if you don't come."

Ella hesitated, chewing on the end of her pen. "I really have a lot to do—"

"Nonsense!" Grandma said, tugging the pen out of her hand. "You can finish your schoolwork later. Let's go make some memories."

I grinned at Ella. "Don't worry, I've been looking forward to the weekend more than anything! I can relax enough for both of us."

Ella rolled her eyes but eventually gave in. "Fine," she said, closing her books. "But just for a little while."

And that's how we all ended up at the pumpkin patch. Even Skelfie came along—mostly because I didn't trust him at home alone...

The moment we arrived, I knew this wasn't going to be as boring as I'd thought. The air smelled like warm apple cider and doughnuts, and before we'd even made it to the entrance, Grandma handed me and Ella each a doughnut.

It was the best thing I'd ever eaten.

Skelfie and the Spookeville Circus

Grandpa tried to sneak Lola a piece, but Grandma caught him. "No sweets for dogs, Harold!" she scolded, swiping the doughnut crumb out of his hand. Grandpa winked at me and ate the rest of his treat himself.

We climbed onto a tractor-pulled wagon that took us out to the pumpkin field. Lola sat on Grandma's lap, looking like a little queen surveying her kingdom. The field stretched out as far as I could see, with pumpkins of every size scattered everywhere.

"You each get to pick one," Grandpa said. "Make it a good one!"

Ella, being Ella, immediately went into full analysis mode. She crouched, inspected stems, and muttered things like, "This one's a bit lopsided," and "The surface isn't smooth enough." I didn't think pumpkins were supposed to be smooth, but whatever.

I ran around until I spotted a massive pumpkin near the edge of the field. I tried to lift it, but it was heavier than I expected. "Grandpa!" I called. "Can you help me roll this thing?"

He jogged over and laughed when he saw my choice. "Going for the biggest one, huh? Good call!" Together, we rolled it to the wagon.

Ella finally picked a perfectly round, medium-sized pumpkin. "This will be easier to carve," she explained.

"Boring," I said. "Mine's way cooler."

"You're ridiculous," she shot back, but I could see her smiling.

Lola sniffed a tiny pumpkin and started pawing at it like she was trying to claim it. Grandma laughed and added it to the wagon. "Looks like Lola's getting one too."

After the pumpkin picking, we went to the apple orchard. Ella carefully selected the best-looking apples, while I tried climbing a tree to grab one from the top. Grandpa spotted me and called out, "Careful, kiddo, or you'll be part of the pie!"

Once our baskets were full, we headed to the barn shop, where Grandma bought a pumpkin pie, an apple pie, and a jar of apple butter. Grandpa patted his stomach and joked, "At this rate, we'll need a second car just to roll me home."

On the way back, I fell asleep in the car with Skelfie and Lola snuggled up on my lap. When I woke up, Ella was jotting something in her notebook—probably planning her pumpkin design. I don't know what mine's going to look like yet, but I'm sure it'll be awesome.

Day 8: October 25th

Maths was the absolute worst today. I had to do this online quiz about fractions, and it was a disaster. For some reason, the program kept glitching, and every time I got an answer wrong, it played this annoying "sad trombone" sound. It wasn't just a little "womp-womp" either—it was loud, like it wanted to embarrass me.

Ella breezed past me with her pile of colour-coded notebooks and said, "Fractions are easy. Just think of them as slices of pie." Easy for her to say. She wasn't the one trying to figure out what 27 divided by three-quarters was while the trombone of doom laughed at her.

Grandpa poked his head in when he heard the sound and said, "Sounds like someone needs a snack break!" He wasn't wrong.

I abandoned the quiz, stomped downstairs, and stuffed my face with Grandma's homemade choc chip biscuits. Skelfie sat at the end of the table, watching me. I almost felt like I should offer him a biscuit, just to keep him happy. But toys can't eat biscuits, right?

After lunch, the day finally got fun. Grandpa said it was time to set up the *Spookeville Circus* decorations in the front yard. He had a whole plan, and he was very excited about it.

"First things first," Grandpa said, clapping his hands together. "We need to set the stage."

Grandma helped him drag out a big box from the garage. Inside were all sorts of decorations: strings of colourful lights, a cardboard ticket booth, and this HUGE plastic skeleton clown with glowing red eyes. "This one's been scaring kids since 1988," Grandpa said proudly.

Ella and I got to work hanging the lights while Grandpa assembled the ticket booth. He kept muttering, "Lefty-loosey, righty-tighty," while twisting the screws, which made me laugh.

The best part was the centrepiece: a giant spooky circus tent made out of purple, black, and orange striped fabric Grandma had sewn herself. She told us she'd originally made it for a Halloween carnival when Mum and Uncle Ben were little. Grandpa set it up in the middle of the yard, and Ella and I helped anchor it with stakes. It looked amazing.

"Now for the stars of the show!" Grandpa said. He pulled out more skeletons—there was a strongman holding a barbell, a skeleton acrobat posed mid-flip, and even a skeleton dog that looked suspiciously like Lola.

"Lola, it's your twin!" I said, holding up the skeleton dog. Lola barked at it like it was a real intruder, which made all of us laugh.

Skelfie and the Spookeville Circus

By the time we were done, the yard looked incredible. The circus tent glowed under the string lights, and the skeletons were all perfectly posed. Grandpa added one last touch: a *Spookeville Circus* sign he'd painted himself.

"Think this will get the neighbourhood's attention?" Grandpa asked, grinning.

"For sure," Ella said. "It's awesome."

We stood there for a moment, admiring our work. Then Grandma said, "Okay, who's ready for toffee apples?" I couldn't help but think of the choc chip biscuits I'd eaten earlier, and how Mum would say that was way too much sugar for one day. But Mum wasn't here, and as much as I missed them sometimes, I was definitely going to take advantage of toffee apples!

Best. Monday. Ever.

Day 9: October 26th

Today was the worst. First, I had to write a summary of *Sarah, Plain and Tall* for my English class. Why couldn't we read something exciting, like a superhero story where the hero battles an evil robot, or a mystery with a secret hidden treasure?

Nope.

Instead, I had to write about the prairie and how Sarah felt about moving there. For the record, I think Sarah wouldn't like my summary because I ended it with, "The prairie is boring, and so is this book."

Grandma raised her eyebrows when she saw it. "Ella's upstairs writing an essay on *To Kill a Mockingbird*," she said. "Maybe you could try putting in as much effort as she does."

"Ugh," I said, slouching over the table. It wasn't like I wanted to do a bad job. The book just wasn't that interesting, and Ella was practically a walking library. Not a fair comparison!

Then history made everything worse. We had to make timelines of important events from the American Revolution. Do you know how many battles there were? Too many. My teacher wanted us to include five with dates, locations, and outcomes. FIVE. It took me forever to figure out if the Battle of Saratoga came before or after the Boston Tea Party. (Spoiler: it's after.)

While I was staring at my notes and wishing I could go outside, Grandpa shuffled in and peered over my shoulder. "That looks interesting!" he said, pointing at a crooked line I'd drawn between the Battle of Bunker Hill and the Declaration of Independence.

"Sure, Grandpa," I muttered. "If by 'interesting' you mean the most boring thing ever."

Skelfie and the Spookeville Circus

He chuckled and patted my shoulder. "I've got faith in you. Now, where'd Grandma hide the good chocolate?"

"Check the top cupboard," I said, so distracted that I didn't even tag along to snag a piece for myself.

The whole day felt like it was swallowed up by schoolwork. By the time I finished the timeline, it was already dark outside, and I hadn't done anything fun. No helping with Halloween, no playing fetch with Lola, nothing. Lola didn't care that I was busy, though—she climbed into my lap and licked my face, her tail wagging like she wanted me to know it was okay.

"You're the only one who understands me," I told her. She barked in agreement.

Tomorrow, I have to find time for Halloween fun. If only I could get Skelfie to do my homework for me. Although he might do even worse than me, on purpose, just to trick me! Oh well, I'll do the work quickly because it's time to focus on the important stuff: Halloween!

Day 10: October 27th

Today was so much fun! Grandma said we were going to make Halloween treats, but first, I had to finish my schoolwork. My music teacher assigned us to watch this really long video about the orchestra and then write a reflection on the conductor's role.

I tried to focus, but honestly, the only thing I could picture was Grandpa waving his arms around like a conductor, cracking jokes between every song. He'd probably say something like, "That's not a bassoon, it's a buffoon! Get it?" and then laugh so hard he'd have to sit down.

Skelfie and the Spookeville Circus

I kept giggling while I typed, and then Ella walked in. She crossed her arms and frowned. "Why aren't you taking this seriously?" she asked, like she was the boss of me or something.

"It's homework, not heart surgery," I said, but she just rolled her eyes.

When Grandma heard me laughing, she peeked over my shoulder. "Maybe you could *conduct* yourself a little better," she said with a grin. Grandpa overheard her and burst out laughing so loud I think he scared Lola, who barked at him like she was telling him to calm down.

Finally, I finished my homework, and it was time to make treats! Grandma had all the ingredients ready in the kitchen. She said we were making Halloween sugar biscuits and cupcakes with spooky decorations.

Ella measured everything perfectly, of course, while I tried to crack an egg one-handed like I'd seen on TV. It didn't go great. Eggshells and goo everywhere. "Oops," I said.

Grandma just laughed and handed me a tea towel. "A little mess never hurt anyone," she said. "But next time, maybe try two hands?"

While the biscuits baked, we started on the cupcake decorations. Grandma had orange and purple icing, candy eyes, and black liquorice for spider legs. She showed us how to pipe icing onto the cupcakes, but my first try looked more like a blob than a pumpkin.

"It's a modern art pumpkin," I said. Ella rolled her eyes again, but Grandma said it was creative.

Grandpa wandered in to "supervise" and ended up eating two plain cupcakes before we could even decorate them. "Quality control," he said with his mouth full.

By the time we finished, the kitchen looked like Halloween had exploded. There was icing on the bench, flour on the floor, and somehow I even got sprinkles in my hair. But the biscuits and cupcakes turned out amazing. We made spider cupcakes, monster biscuits with candy eyes, and even some mummy-shaped ones with white icing "bandages." Lola kept circling the kitchen like she was hoping we'd drop something, but Grandma shooed her out and said, "No sweets for dogs!"

After everything was cleaned up, we sat down to taste our treats. When we were done, Ella said the spider cupcakes looked too real, which made me laugh and reminded me of when she screamed earlier when I pretended one was crawling toward her.

When she left the room, I took Grandma aside for a top secret conversation about our Halloween costumes. Her eyes sparkled after I told her what I had in mind, and she said she would get to work—secretly, of course!

Halloween is getting closer, and it's turning out to be the best one ever.

Skelfie and the Spookeville Circus

Day 11: October 28th

I'm writing this from under my blankets because I can't stop thinking about Grandma's ghost story. I'm so scared, I can't even sleep! I keep looking at the shadows in my room, and every creak of the house sounds like a ghost creeping down the hall.

It all started after dinner when Grandpa said, "Who's up for some ghost stories?" He turned off the lights in the lounge room and lit a few candles. The flickering made everything look spooky, especially the old photos on the walls.

I sat on the couch next to Lola, who snuggled up like she wasn't afraid of anything. Grandpa started with a story about a ghostly hitchhiker who disappears when the driver asks where she lives. I laughed because Grandpa made silly ghost noises and waved his arms like he was trying to scare us. It wasn't scary, but it was funny watching him get so into it.

Then I told a story I remembered from a campfire last summer. It was about a haunted doll that moves on its own. I tried to make my voice all low and creepy, and Grandpa said, "Ooooh, spooky!" but I could tell he wasn't scared.

Ella came in then, holding a book like she wasn't interested. "What are you doing?" she asked, raising an eyebrow.

"Telling ghost stories," I said. "Want to try?"

She rolled her eyes but sat down anyway. "Fine. I'll tell one."

Her story was about a scientist who creates a monster that escapes and terrorises the town. She went on and on about experiments and electricity, using big words like *galvanised* and *synapse*.

When she finished, Grandpa clapped. "Bravo, Ella! I feel like I just got a science lesson. Spooky stuff!"

"It wasn't scary," I said. "Just kind of... smart."

Ella smirked. "Not my fault if you don't get it."

Then Grandma came in with her knitting and said, "You call those ghost stories? Let me tell you a real one."

We all leaned in as she set her knitting aside and started talking in a soft, low voice. She told us about a woman who moves into an old house. At night, she hears footsteps in the attic, even though no one else is home. One night, she goes up to check, and when she opens the attic door, she sees...

Grandma paused, her eyes wide. "She sees a figure, pale and thin, with long, bony fingers. It turns to her, and its eyes are empty black pits!"

She made a sudden grabbing motion, and we all screamed—yes, even Ella! Lola barked and hid under the blanket on my lap. Grandpa was laughing so hard he had to wipe his eyes, but even he admitted, "That one gave me chills, love."

I tried to act brave, but I couldn't stop thinking about the attic ghost. Even when we turned the lights back on, I kept looking over my shoulder...

Skelfie was sitting on top of the TV! I know he wasn't there when we started telling the ghost stories. Had Grandma summoned him when she described the bony creature?

Now I'm in bed, and every little noise makes me jump. Is that just the wind? Or is it footsteps? I had to turn Uncle Ben's Skelfie to face the wall because I think he was watching me. I should've left him where he was on the TV because I swear he watched me walk across the room to get to bed. I really wish Lola could sleep in here with me tonight. I think I'll leave my nightlight on... just in case.

Skelfie and the Spookeville Circus

Day 12: October 29th

Today didn't go quite as planned. Grandpa wasn't feeling well, so we didn't get much work done on the Halloween decorations. That was disappointing because we were supposed to put up the big spider web across the porch and hang the glowing bats from the tree. Grandpa said we still have plenty of time, but I'm starting to worry. Two days doesn't feel like much when you've got an entire haunted yard to finish!

Instead, Grandma and I spent most of the morning in the kitchen, working on more Halloween treats. We made sugar lollies shaped like pumpkins and ghosts. Those are my favourite because they're so sweet, and the pumpkin ones are covered in sparkly orange sugar. We also made another tray of chocolate fudge and caramel slice, which takes forever because you have to wait for the caramel to cool before cutting it.

When we were done, Grandma had me pack up the earlier treats we'd made into little clear bags tied with ribbons. She said the neighbours were going to love them, and I felt pretty proud of how nice everything looked. I was imagining how surprised the neighbourhood kids would be when they saw all the treats—until I went back to the kitchen.

Some of the lollies were missing.

"Grandma," I said, staring at the empty spot on the tray. "Did you already pack the sugar lollies?"

Grandma looked confused. "No, dear. Not yet. Why?"

I pointed. "There were ten pumpkin lollies right there. And... wait—" I counted quickly. "The caramel's missing a few pieces too!"

Grandma frowned, wiping her hands on her apron. "Are you sure you didn't eat some?"

"Me? No way!" I protested. "I've only had one piece all morning!"

That's when Lola came trotting in, her little nose sniffing the air like she was looking for food. She had the most innocent expression, but her tail wagged like she was hiding something.

"Lola!" I groaned. "Did you eat the treats?"

Lola just wagged harder, tilting her head like she had no idea what I was talking about.

Grandma crouched down and looked at the counter. "Oh, dear. I didn't think she could reach up there. Do you think she got into them somehow?"

Skelfie and the Spookeville Circus

We both turned and looked at the chair by the counter. It was slightly pushed out—just enough for a sneaky dachshund to hop up and stretch her little legs toward the treats.

"Lola, you little rascal!" I said.

Grandma sighed but smiled. "Well, I suppose it's partly my fault for not moving them farther out of reach. Let's hope she didn't eat too much, or we'll have one very hyper pup on our hands."

Speaking of not feeling well, Grandpa stayed in his lounge chair most of the day with a blanket and a cup of tea. When Grandma told him about the missing treats, he chuckled weakly. "Maybe it wasn't Lola. Maybe there's a Halloween ghost sneaking around the house!"

"Or Skelfie!" I said, but both grandparents just waved off my worry.

Now I'm lying here in bed, wondering if Skelfie loves sweets or just likes to cause trouble however he can.

Lilli Adams

Day 13: October 30th

This morning, Grandpa was feeling much better, which was a relief because today we got to take a walk around the neighbourhood to check out all the Halloween decorations.

Ella didn't want to go at first—she said she had homework to finish—but Grandma told her, "You need some fresh air before you turn into one of those skeletons everyone's putting up." That made us all laugh, and Ella finally grabbed her hoodie and came along.

The first yard we stopped at had this huge skeleton, at least twelve feet tall. Someone had put a purple witch's hat on its head and tied a broom to one of its hands. It looked like it was about to sweep the leaves off the lawn—or swat someone sneaking past.

"Imagine that thing coming to life," I said, stepping closer to get a better look.

"Imagine it chasing you!" Grandpa added, making his hands into claws.

I laughed nervously, but I took a step back. You never know with Halloween decorations.

The next house was one of my favourites. The whole front yard was turned into a creepy graveyard with crooked tombstones, skeletons poking out of the ground, and cobwebs everywhere. A fog machine pumped out little clouds that drifted around the gravestones. One of the skeletons was holding a shovel, like it had just dug its own grave.

"Clever," Ella said. "But wouldn't the skeleton be in the grave, not digging it?"

"It's probably digging for a better plot," Grandpa joked with a wink.

Ella groaned. "Grandpa, no."

Skelfie and the Spookeville Circus

I laughed despite myself. Grandpa loves a good pun—even if they're painfully bad!

At another house, there was a witch decoration that looked like she had flown straight into a tree. Her broomstick was sticking out one side of the trunk, and her legs and arms were flattened against the bark. Someone had even added a little sign that said, "Don't text and fly!" Grandpa took about ten photos of it, laughing so hard he could barely hold his phone steady.

Then we got to the creepiest one. There was a small skeleton sitting on a tyre swing, hanging from an old oak tree. At first, I thought it was just sitting there, but then the wind started blowing, and the swing moved back and forth. The skeleton's bony arms jiggled as if it was holding on tight, and its head bobbed like it was watching us.

"I think it's looking at me," I whispered.

"It's not real," Ella said, rolling her eyes. "It's just the wind."

But I swear, as we walked away, I felt like the skeleton's hollow eye sockets were following us.

When we got back to Grandma and Grandpa's house, we decided to have a scary movie marathon. Grandma made us a platter of Halloween-themed snacks: peeled grapes in a bowl that she said were "eyeballs," string cheese sticks with little faces drawn on them to look like ghosts, popcorn with lolly corn mixed in, and tiny sandwiches cut into bat shapes.

We set everything up in the lounge room, dimmed the lights, and turned on the first movie. Lola curled up on Grandma's lap, snoring softly while the rest of us screamed at the jump scares. I pulled Skelfie close to me, just in case he could offer some protection.

By the time the third movie ended, my stomach was full of popcorn and lollies, and my eyes were heavy. Grandpa wanted to keep watching, but Ella and I called it a night. As I climbed into bed, I thought about that skeleton on the swing again. I tried to convince myself it was just a decoration, but a little voice in my head whispered, *What if it wasn't?*

Tomorrow's Halloween, and now I don't know if I'm ready for it!

Day 14: October 31st - Halloween

This morning started with the best surprise ever: Grandma had fixed Uncle Ben's old "Skelfie" costume and made a new costume for Skelfie himself. It's funny how a new costume can make you feel special. Even Skelfie's expression looked different, which was basically impossible because he's just a toy... or is he?!

Sundays are usually a little slower, but not today. There was no school, no homework, and no boring Zoom lessons—just Halloween, waiting for us to dive in.

When I woke up, I could already smell something amazing coming from the kitchen. I bounded downstairs and found Grandma humming as she whisked what looked like pancake batter, wearing a sparkling blue dress with glittery stars all over it.

"Good morning, pumpkin," she said with a wink. "Or should I say, 'future ringmaster extraordinaire'?"

"Are you a princess?" I asked.

"I'm your Fairy Grandmother," she said, giving me a twirl. The skirt flared out, and I noticed she'd even pinned a tiny wand charm into her hair. "I thought I'd sprinkle a little magic into our day."

"Grandma, you already did! This is awesome!" I grinned as she handed me a stack of pancakes shaped like bats and pumpkins.

After breakfast, she took me upstairs to show me the costume. I couldn't believe my eyes. Uncle Ben's old ringmaster jacket looked brand new. Grandma had sewn on shiny gold buttons to the sparkly orange vest. On the back of the black jacket, a little skeleton with a grey top hat grinned at me, making me laugh. I would be dressed like Skelfie while wearing a picture of him too!

I ran to try it on, and it fit perfectly. The jacket felt snug but comfortable, and the little details—like the purple lapels—made it feel like the best costume ever.

When I came downstairs in my costume, Grandpa was already waiting in his. He stood in the lounge room, spinning his cane like a pro. "Step right up! Behold the amazing ringmaster duo!" he announced, bowing so low his hat almost fell off.

I couldn't stop laughing. Grandpa's vest was even shinier than mine, and his top hat had a raven's feather sticking out of it. He handed me a matching cane topped with a jack-o'-lantern, and we practised our "ringmaster stances" for at least ten minutes.

Skelfie and the Spookeville Circus

Ella, who was usually glued to a book on Sunday mornings, actually closed it to watch us. "You two are going to scare the lollies out of the neighbours," she said, rolling her eyes but smiling anyway.

"You should dress up too," I said.

"I'm good, thanks," Ella replied, but Grandma wasn't having it.

"Oh, come now," Grandma said, walking into the room and waving her hands like a real fairy godmother. "Every witch needs a hat." She pulled out a tall, slightly crooked black hat from behind her back and plonked it onto Ella's head.

Ella groaned but didn't take it off. "Fine, but only because it matches my jumper."

"Witchy perfection," Grandpa said, giving her a thumbs-up.

We spent the rest of the morning decorating the front yard. Grandpa had carved extra pumpkins the night before, and now they sat on the porch glowing with candles inside. Lola, who was zooming around in her tiny lion costume, tried to "attack" the fake cobwebs we were hanging.

By the time we finished, the yard looked amazing. I could already feel the excitement building for tonight. Halloween was finally here, and it was going to be the best one ever.

After an early dinner, Ella and I got ready for trick-or-treating. I grabbed my little pumpkin bucket, which went perfectly with the jack-o'-lantern on top of my cane, and we headed out.

The neighbourhood was buzzing with kids in costume. Some were dressed as superheroes, others as princesses, and a group of kids had coordinated outfits as a box of crayons. We joined up with a group of kids around my age who were already making their way down the street.

Lilli Adams

The first house we stopped at had a giant inflatable ghost that glowed in the dark. A woman dressed as a pirate handed out full-sized chocolate bars, which immediately made her house the favourite.

"Full-sized Snickers? This is the jackpot!" I said, grinning at Ella.

"Don't eat it all at once," she warned. "Grandma will make you eat boiled cabbage tomorrow if you get a stomach-ache."

At another house, a man dressed as Frankenstein handed out lollies from a cauldron. One kid in a mummy costume jumped back when a hidden skeleton popped out from behind the cauldron.

We passed the house with the graveyard decorations, which somehow looked even creepier at night. The fog machine was working overtime, and the skeleton with the shovel had glowing red eyes.

"Those eyes are following us," I whispered to Ella.

"It's just lights," she said, but I noticed she kept glancing back at it as we walked away.

The last house we stopped at had a little haunted trail in the front yard. There were hanging ghosts, a werewolf with glowing yellow eyes, and a zombie that crawled out of the bushes when you got too close. I screamed, but so did Ella, which made me laugh so hard I dropped my pumpkin bucket.

"Don't you dare tell Grandpa I screamed," she said, helping me pick up my lollies.

When we got back home, Grandpa had turned our yard into his own little haunted house. He was waiting on the porch in his ringmaster costume, holding a torch under his chin to make his face look eerie. Lola was running around in a tiny lion costume, barking at everything.

Skelfie and the Spookeville Circus

Grandma had set up a table with her famous Halloween biscuits shaped like bats and pumpkins. There were also toffee apples and little bags of popcorn with chocolate chips mixed in.

Kids from the neighbourhood lined up to go through our "haunted yard." Grandpa led them down a path lined with flickering jack-o'-lanterns and fake cobwebs. I hid behind one of the bushes since I was dressed as Skelfie, jumping out to scare them when they least expected it.

Ella even joined in, handing out lollies while pretending to be a grumpy witch. One little kid asked her if she was a real witch, and she smirked and said, "Only on weekdays."

By the end of the night, my cheeks hurt from laughing, and Grandpa had lost his voice from all his ringmaster announcements. It was the best Halloween ever!

Lilli Adams

Epilogue:
November 1st - All Saints' Day

My parents came to pick us up today, and I tried really hard not to think about how tomorrow everything goes back to normal—school, homework, boring stuff. For now, I just want to think about Halloween and how it was the BEST one ever.

The first thing I did when they walked through the door (after giving them big hugs, of course) was pull them into the lounge room to show off the photos Grandma took.

"So, this is me and Grandpa in our matching ringmaster costumes," I said, pointing to the first picture. I looked pretty cool with my orange vest and gold bow tie, and Grandpa was twirling his cane mid-pose like he was actually running a circus.

Dad grinned. "I love it! You look like you're about to introduce the greatest show on Earth."

"Wait till you see the yard!" I flipped to the next picture, which showed the front yard glowing in the dark. The giant spider web we'd hung stretched from the porch to the tree, and the glowing bats looked like they were flying through the fog machine Grandpa had rigged to blow puffs every few minutes.

Mum gasped. "That's amazing! Did you and Ella help with all of that?"

I nodded proudly. "Yep! Ella was in charge of the skeletons."

Mum shot a proud smile at Ella, who didn't even notice because she was reading a book on the couch.

Next, I showed Mum and Dad the pictures of the *Spookeville Circus*, including the game stations we made. Grandma had decorated a table

Skelfie and the Spookeville Circus

like a carnival booth, and we used hoops for ring toss around pumpkin stems. The kids from the neighbourhood loved it—especially when Grandpa started announcing everyone like they were circus stars.

"This is the one where Skelfie stole the show," I said, holding up my favourite picture. Grandma had fixed up Uncle Ben's skeleton toy, which was sitting in the middle of the table with its little top hat, tiny black jacket, and orange vest. Grandma had set up a spotlight just for him, and it looked like he was running the whole thing.

All the local kids had been mesmerised by Skelfie. We had all these pranks planned that we blamed Skelfie for... though some of the pranks, like when one of the kids found a fake spider inside their lolly bag, we could not explain.

Mum laughed. "I can't believe Grandma still has Skelfie! That's so funny."

"She even fixed his costume," I told her. "And added sparkly patches to match ours. He was like the star of the whole circus."

I spent the rest of the evening telling them everything. By the end, I was so tired I almost fell asleep on the couch.

Now I'm lying in my own bed, thinking about how perfect the last two weeks have been. I know I'll have to go back to regular life tomorrow, but for tonight, I'm holding on to every moment of *Spookeville Circus*.

www.ingramcontent.com/pod-product-compliance
Lightning Source LLC
Chambersburg PA
CBHW061225070526
44584CB00029B/3997